OUTDOORS

PETE SANDERS

GLOUCESTER PRESS
London · New York · Toronto · Sydney

Introduction

There are many places to explore outdoors — playgrounds, streets, parks and the countryside are just a few of them. Some are safer than others. But even when you play in safe places, there may be risks. You have to learn about safety so you know how to look after yourself. The ideas in this book will help to keep you from harm, whenever you are outdoors.

Take a close look at the picture on this page. Some of the children are in dangerous situations. How many of these can you spot? You will find some of the answers at the end of this book on page 29.

OUTDOORS

Designed and produced by
Aladdin Books Ltd, 70 Old Compton Street,
London W1V 5PA

Design: David West
Children's Book Design

Illustrators: Tizzie Knowles, Louise Nevitt

Pete Sanders is the head teacher of a North London
primary school and is working with teachers on
personal, social and health education.

The publishers would like to thank all the children
who posed for the pictures used in this book.

Published in Great Britain in 1989 by
Franklin Watts Ltd, 12a Golden Square,
London W1R 4BA

ISBN 0 86313 954 X

Printed in Belgium

Going outside

There are many safety devices outdoors to keep you safe. Some, like fences, are always there. Others appear when there is a particular danger like road works. Signs warn us about possible dangers. Why don't they have many words on them?

When you go outdoors it's important to wear the right clothes. People who work outdoors often wear special clothes either to protect themselves or to tell us who they are. It is easy to identify the police and fire fighters. When you visit a building site, the foreman will make you wear a hard hat to protect your head. Can you think of safety equipment you might use?

 INFORMATION

When you go outdoors, you often need to wear things to protect you from the climate. On hot days you should wear a hat to guard against the sun. Sunglasses help stop the sun's glare in your eyes. In winter hats keep you from getting cold. When it's snowing you should wear plenty of layers to keep you warm and be careful to cover your fingers and ears. On rainy days you need a strong rainproof coat and hat.

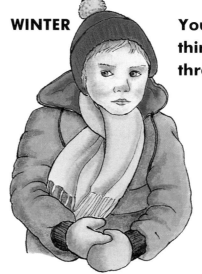

WINTER

Your body can lose one-third of its heat through the head

SUMMER

Your head and shoulders need protection from the sun's harmful rays.

6

The cones have been put there to warn you about the roadworks.

Thinking first

It's always a good idea to think before you act. Sometimes you can forget road safety rules because you're thinking about something else or you're excited about something. Learning to be safe helps you make the right decisions.

When you're playing outside you should make sure you choose a safe place. Can you think of places which would be dangerous to play in? Look at page 5. Some of the children are not playing in safe places. Before going out make sure you're wearing the right clothes and have got the right equipment. Always tell someone where you are going to play. When you get home again, wash yourself carefully.

INFORMATION

Adults often worry about children being out in the dark. One reason for this is because it's more difficult to see and be seen. Wearing bright and light colours or reflective clothing helps you to be seen. Also if you're walking on a road without a footpath, it's best to walk facing the traffic. That means you can always see the traffic that is coming towards you and keep well out of the way.

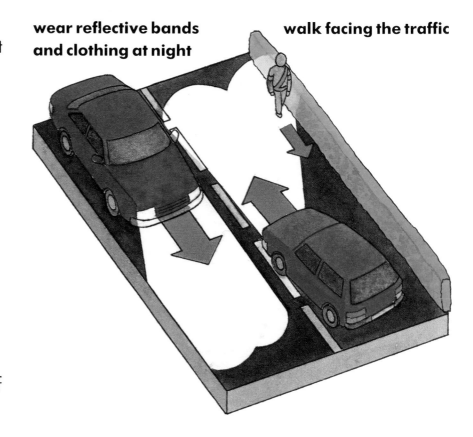

wear reflective bands and clothing at night

walk facing the traffic

Umbrellas are very useful on a rainy day.

Find out what are the best colours to wear in green fields or woods. Take a piece of green card and place other strips of coloured card on top of it. See which colour shows up the best. Get your friends to try it and see if they agree with you. Use some black card to find out what colours show up best in the dark.

9

In the garden

Do you have a garden to play in? If you don't, you may have played in a friend's garden. There are lots of games to play there like football, exploring or digging. You still have to think about safety. You can hurt yourself if you go barefoot. Wearing the right shoes is important. You shouldn't play too near windows in case you break one.

Garden sheds contain a lot of equipment. Only use garden equipment if an adult has shown you what to do. You can run all kinds of risks if you play with things in a shed. Rusty nails or tools can give you dangerous germs if they cut you.

INFORMATION

Here are some of the things you should watch out for in the garden. Don't try to eat a berry before asking an adult. Nettles and thorns can sting and scratch you. Bees and wasps might hurt you if they feel threatened. If one comes near you, stay very still. Some animals, like dogs or foxes, have insects like fleas and mites on them. These can harm your skin. Animal droppings are full of germs.

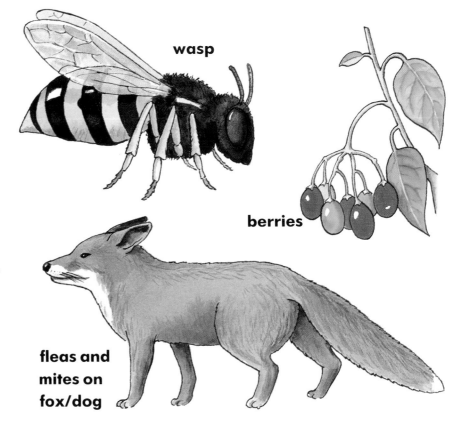

wasp

berries

fleas and mites on fox/dog

Climbing frames are fun to play on but make sure you land carefully.

In the town

Keeping safe means that you have to think about others as well as yourself. People are not always as careful as they should be about protecting others from roadworks, building sites or even rubbish.

We all know that litter should go in bins. Yet people drop objects like bottles and cans on the ground, forgetting that others can trip up and hurt themselves. Some children have been killed by getting locked in an old fridge or crushed by a car on a dump.

You need to be careful getting on and off buses in towns. Don't try to get on a moving bus and don't try to get off in a hurry.

PROJECT

When you do the same journey a lot, you can stop noticing what's around you. Choose a route that you often take – maybe the one from home to school. Take a sheet of paper, and draw a plan of it from beginning to end. Mark on it any places which might be dangerous, both for yourself and for others. You could also mark safe parts too. Show your map to your friends. Do they agree with you?

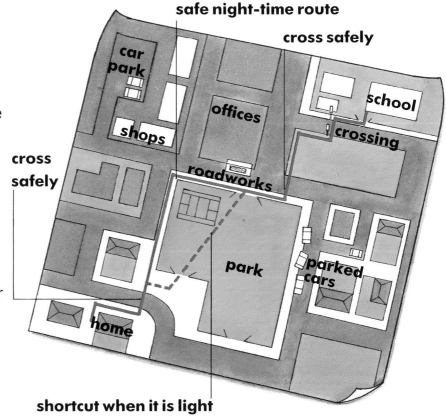

safe night-time route

cross safely

car park

school

offices

shops

crossing

cross safely

roadworks

park

parked cars

home

shortcut when it is light

Only play on streets where no cars are allowed.

Always look at a building site from a safe distance.

How safe are the pavements in your neighbourhood? Are there any holes that need to be fixed? Are there enough litter bins? If you think something should be done about this, write a letter to your town hall or local newspaper.

At the park

Some parks have areas where you can play. This doesn't necessarily make them safe. There may be climbing frames where the ground underneath is very hard or perhaps there are swings which do not have enough space around them. Any park equipment can become dangerous if you don't play on it safely. Don't jump off a slide or a seesaw. Make sure no one gets too close to the swings.

You shouldn't talk to anyone you don't know, even if they are friendly. If an adult offers you sweets or gifts, just say no. There are people around who want to harm children. They may go to a park because that's where children play.

INFORMATION

Parks often have rules. Some don't allow dogs or cyclists. That's so other people can enjoy themselves. Before you go to the park, it's a good idea to find out what you can and can't do there. Stick to the rules. Some rules are not written down but everyone knows them. You shouldn't make noise or have loud music on because it disturbs other people. You have to think about other people's needs as well as your own.

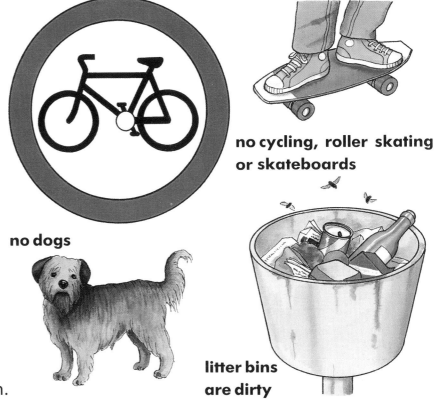

no cycling, roller skating or skateboards

no dogs

litter bins are dirty

This is a safe playground. Can you spot the safety features?

Paddling pools are safe but watch out for younger children.

A country walk

Here are a few things you should check before going for a walk in the country. You need to have an adult you can trust with you. Wear the right clothes and shoes for the time of year. Tell someone what time they should expect you back from the walk. Even if you know the area well, stick with the people in your group. It's not a good idea to wander off on your own.

It's sensible to walk along a footpath in the country. If you do get lost, stop and think carefully about what to do. It might be best to retrace your steps or to ask directions at the nearest house or to head for the nearest road.

INFORMATION

If you come across farm equipment on a walk, leave it alone. When you go through gates, make sure you shut them behind you. Fences are always there for a reason. If you go into a fenced-off area, you may be trespassing and breaking the law. Some fences have an electric current going through. These give shocks to anyone who touches them. Others are made of barbed wire and can hurt you.

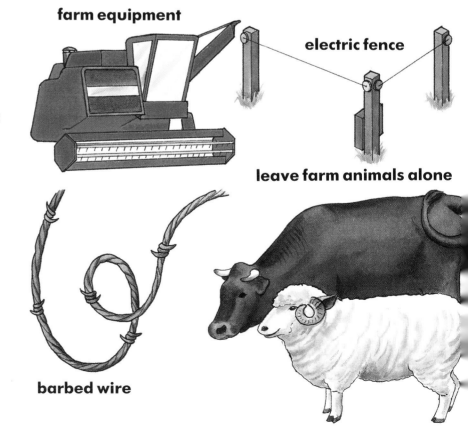

farm equipment

electric fence

leave farm animals alone

barbed wire

16

Wearing the right clothes and boots is very important.

These children could hurt themselves playing near the rubbish on this farm.

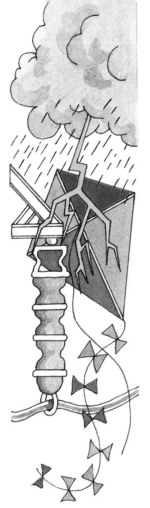

In the country

If you're not used to the countryside there are lots of things you can get caught out by. You have to watch out for changes of weather. Is there likely to be a storm? You should be careful near water and not drink from a stream. There are lots of wild flowers and plants but some of them are poisonous. Even if something looks familiar, don't taste it.

Many children like to stroke animals. This is not a good idea if you don't know the animal. Dogs can be particularly aggressive especially if they have been trained to guard property. Keep well away from them. If you see a snake, stop and move away as quickly as possible.

 ## INFORMATION

Lightning usually strikes the highest point. It's rare for people to get struck, but here are a few safety hints if you are in a storm.

• don't stay in open space or on high ground. Find a ditch.
• keep away from tall trees which may get struck.
• keep away from metal fences.
• you shouldn't fly a kite, ride a bike or a horse in a storm.

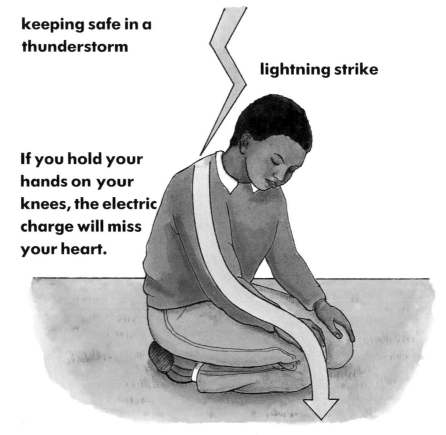

keeping safe in a thunderstorm

lightning strike

If you hold your hands on your knees, the electric charge will miss your heart.

You can get swept along by fast flowing water so keep well away.

Stroking animals you don't know is not a good idea.

Going camping

You should only go camping with experienced campers. They will know what equipment to take and where is the best place to put up a tent. The best spot is where there is flat ground, away from water and sheltered from the wind. You need to test the ground to see how firm it is and check that there are no stones below the surface.

It's sensible to listen to weather forecasts. If heavy rains are expected, you should dig channels to carry water away from the tent. In strong wind put stones on the pegs and flaps. If there are very strong winds, it's best to find some other kind of shelter.

INFORMATION

If you are going on a camping trip, you need to be prepared for all weathers. That is why it's important to have clothes that are waterproof and windproof. Having the right kind of footwear is important too. You should have some spare clothes and shoes. Other useful bits of equipment are a good torch, a first aid kit and a compass. A compass will help you follow a map in open country.

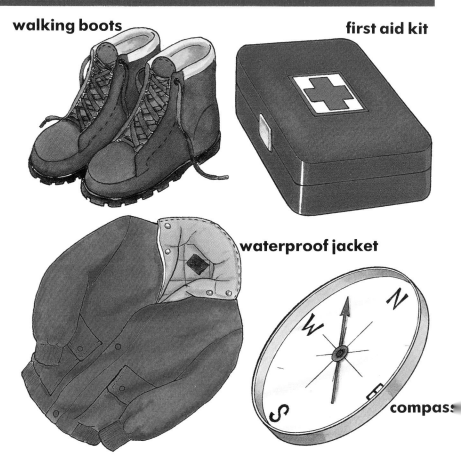

walking boots

first aid kit

waterproof jacket

compass

These children are pitching their tent on level ground.

This is a safe way to use a knife.

Before setting out, good campers make a list of things they need to take with them. What would you take? Make a list and write why they are important. For example, a compass for finding directions, a whistle to call for help.

Going by train

When you're on a train watch out for the doors. Some can be opened when the train is moving. Sometimes people open the door before the train has stopped. This is very dangerous.

When trains pass each other they get very close, so you should never lean out of the window. Passengers who travel alone often look for a carriage with a lot of people in it. If there is a problem there is a communication button which can be used in an emergency.

Accidents don't only happen on trains. Some children have been badly hurt because they forgot the rule which says that you shouldn't go on railway property.

PROJECT

Level crossings close when a signal is sent to them that a train is approaching. You can make your own level crossing gate using some card, a magnet, a drinking straw, some lollipop sticks, a drawing pin, some pins and some plasticine. Attach the magnet to a small piece of card. Make the gate as shown in the drawing. If you slide the magnet under the gate it will make the gate open.

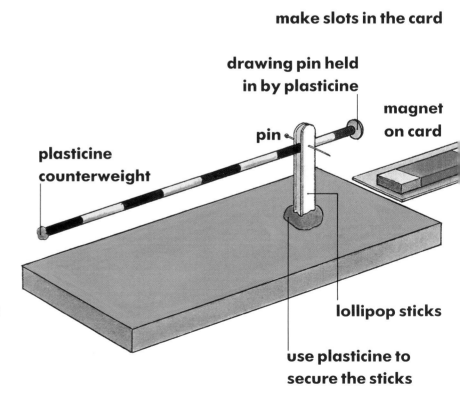

make slots in the card

drawing pin held in by plasticine

magnet on card

pin

plasticine counterweight

lollipop sticks

use plasticine to secure the sticks

It's best to stand well clear of the platform edge.

draw road markings

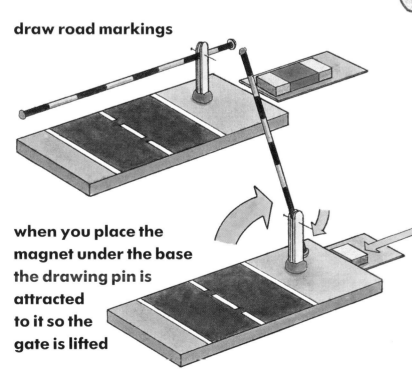

when you place the magnet under the base the drawing pin is attracted to it so the gate is lifted

Train journeys can be fun if you take an interest in the route. Before starting out, draw a map of your route. Make symbols for things you might see on your journey, like a town, bridge, tunnel or farm. Put them in when you see them. You could play this game with your friends.

23

Avoiding risks

Nobody wants to get hurt, so it's important to know how to stay safe outdoors. You need to think about risks and risk-taking. People get hurt when they take risks. Daring others to do something can put them in a difficult situation. You have to make up your own mind about whether a risk is worth taking or not. It's better to say no to a dare than to get hurt, even if it means that others might make fun of you.

It's also important to be prepared for emergencies. For example, it's not a good idea to try to learn how to read a map when you are lost. Doing this beforehand will help to keep you safe.

PROJECT

Make a list of some of the risky things that children and adults do. For example, taking a shortcut through a field or walking round roadworks. Write down if it is very dangerous or just a little. Ask your friends to do the same and see if you agree with each other. Make a poster of some of the most risky things which shows why they are risky. Use it as a reminder to think before taking any high-risk activities.

Can you think of any others?

This boy is taking a risk going so close to the edge.

Thinking of others

Now that you know more about safety outdoors, you should be able to think of how you can help others. There may be dangers that you know about. It can be very helpful to tell someone about them. Accidents often happen because people have not thought carefully enough about what they are doing. You can easily startle other people if you are out on a bike or skateboarding or just playing around. Don't do anything unexpected which will put others at risk or make them panic.

Younger children often copy older children. If you do things with safety in mind, you will be setting a good example.

PROJECT

You probably know one of the symbols for dangerous chemicals. It's a skull and crossbones. Think of some of the dangerous things that can happen to people outdoors, like tripping over in a playground or slipping down a muddy hill. Try to design symbols to warn others of the dangers. Once you have done this, show it to your friends. Do they understand what your signs mean?

weather warning

Can you think of more signs?

If you have to go through a barbed wire fence be very careful.

By remembering to close a gate, you can make sure animals do not escape.

Safety game

After many accidents, people often say that they didn't mean them to happen. This is probably true. It's just that they forgot to think, or they haven't learned any better yet.

Try to think of fun ways in which you can help others to think about keeping safe outdoors. You might make up a safety song or draw some cartoon pictures. Or you could make your own safety board game.

PROJECT

You might want to try out the game opposite. To make it you will need some card, something to draw and colour with, some scissors and a ruler. You will need to draw out your board. On the one opposite the players go from the town to the park and then the countryside. You can write in your own rules, for example, go back to the start if you play near a railway line. Instead of using flat counters, you can make little people. Make sure that they are the right size to fit the squares of your board.

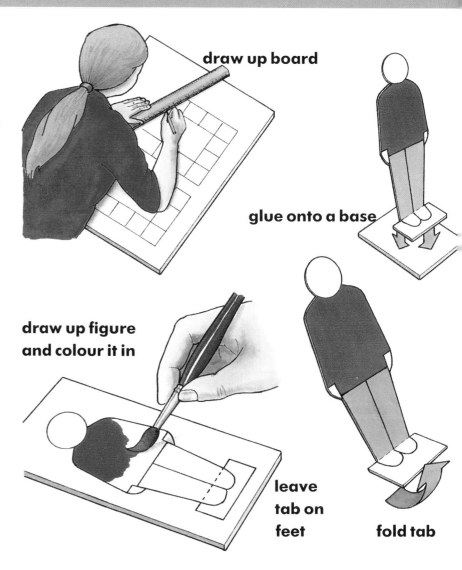

draw up board

glue onto a base

draw up figure and colour it in

leave tab on feet

fold tab

CAN YOU THINK OF MORE HAZARDS?

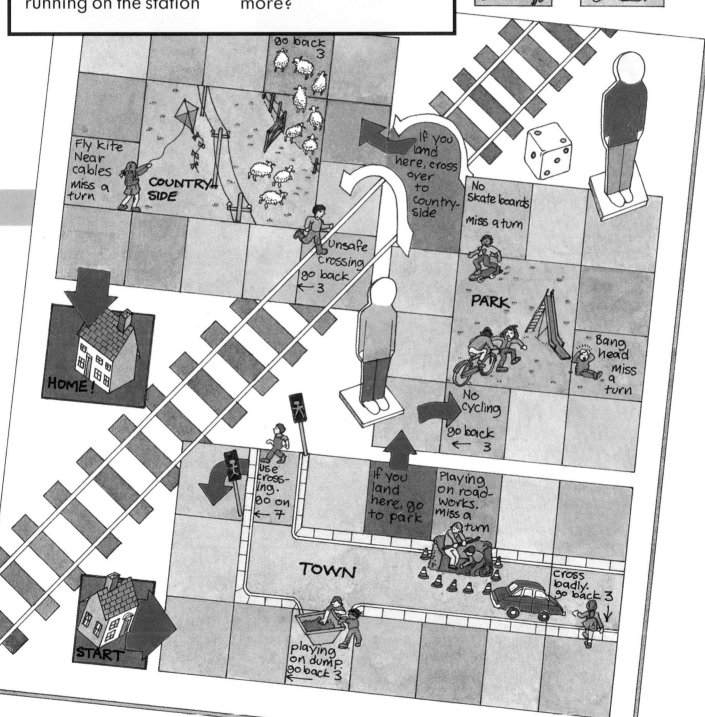

First Aid

First aid is giving care and help to someone who is hurt. You need to have lessons to be good at first aid. The ideas here are to help you to know what to do if you hurt yourself or if you come across somebody who needs some help. Reading this section does not make you into an expert.

Taking a pulse

Taking someone's pulse will tell you how fast the heart is beating. The speed varies according to a person's age and what he or she has been doing. The rate for a 10-year-old child is about 90 beats a minute. For an adult who has been running it would be 140 beats a minute. A normal pulse is regular and strong. Anything else indicates a problem. The best place to take a pulse is the wrist. Place two fingers on the inside of the wrist and press gently. Count the beats for a minute.

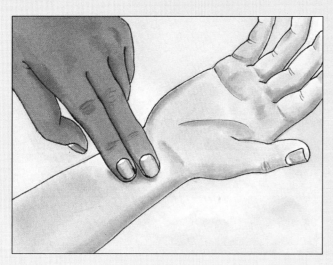

A nosebleed

A nosebleed can happen for many reasons. People with nosebleeds should loosen anything that is tight around the neck and chest. He should sit with his head slightly forward to stop the blood going into the throat.

The nostrils should be pinched for 10 minutes. If this doesn't work, you should do the same thing for another 10 minutes. If the bleeding stops, the nose should not be blown for at least four hours.

If a nosebleed won't stop, it's best to get a doctor. Remember that seeing a lot of blood is frightening to some people.

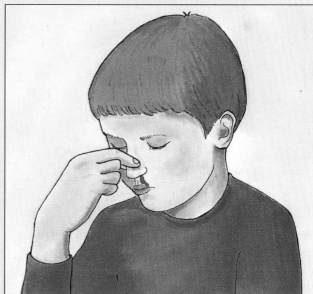

Cuts

If someone has a cut that won't stop bleeding, pressing on it will stop the flow of blood. Make sure dirt doesn't get into the cut and cover it with a clean piece of material.

Sprains

If someone has a sprained ankle, it's best to take off the shoe, and raise the foot. Take an ice pack or a cloth that has been put under a cold water tap and squeezed out. Wrap it around the sprained area and keep it in place for at least 30 minutes to stop the swelling. Afterwards, the sprain should be bandaged firmly.

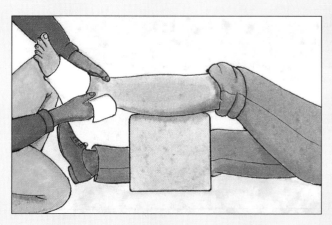

As with all first aid, getting adult help is essential. This is important with sprains, as it can be hard to tell the difference between a sprain and a fracture.

Frostbite

Frostbite happens when the ears, nose, chin, hands and feet are in the cold for too long. It can cause prickling pain and numbness.

If someone has frost bite, find shelter for her. Take off any clothing from the affected area. You should warm the frostbite gradually by skin to skin contact. Use your hands or armpits. Then wrap the area in cloth and cover it with a blanket.

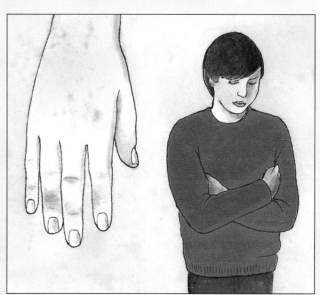

Emergency

- Keep a clear head and don't panic.
- Don't put yourself in danger.
- Think of a way of getting help at once.
- If it is necessary, dial 999. The call is free.
- Know what kind of help you want – the police, the ambulance or the fire brigade.
- Be ready to give the phone number you are using, and to explain where you are.
- You will need to explain how the accident happened.
- Don't put the telephone down until the person that you are talking to has finished.

- When you are outdoors try to remember where the nearest phone box is.

Index

Photographic Credits:
Cover and pages 11, 17t, 19 both and 21 both: Tim and Jenny Woodcock; pages 7, 9, 13b, 15t, 23 and 27b: Marie-Helene Bradley; page 13t: Frank Spooner Agency; pages 15b and 25: Spectrum Colour Library; pages 17b and 27t: Aladdin Pictures.

PRINTED IN BELGIUM BY

proost
INTERNATIONAL BOOK PRODUCTION